THE
INSTANT POT® DESSERTS COOKBOOK

DEVELOPED BY

WILLIAMS SONOMA
TEST KITCHEN

Photographs Erin Scott

weldon**owen**

CONTENTS

Cinnamon-Sugar Monkey Bread
(page 31)

Introduction

The Instant Pot®, which debuted in 2009, quickly became a wildly popular countertop kitchen appliance, winning millions of enthusiastic fans eager to praise its ability to cut cooking time, turn tough cuts of meat fork-tender, and cook such mealtime staples as beans and grains with just the press of a button. Master the basic functions of this whisper-silent, electric, programmable pressure cooker, its admirers say, and you can give away your pressure cooker, slow cooker, and rice cooker because the Instant Pot® can do everything they can—and more.

Sauté, stew, steam, pressure cook, slow cook—the Instant Pot® does them all for breakfast, lunch, and dinner. And its versatility doesn't stop at omelets, risottos, chilis, and other savory recipes. This indispensable pot also offers up a robust repertoire of dinnertime desserts and daytime sweets that rivals what's possible with both conventional ovens and stove-top cooking. With just a couple of basic functions, you can cook a rich cheesecake in about a half hour, a sticky-sweet monkey bread in just over twenty minutes, and creamy rice pudding in less than five minutes.

What's more, the Instant Pot®, with its smart sensors and precision timing, takes the guesswork out of "baking." While a conventional oven too often produces a sunken or cracked cheesecake and dry-crumbed cakes and sweet breads, the controlled steam of an Instant Pot® delivers silky-smooth cheesecakes and dense, moist cakes and breads every time. In the following pages, you'll find a primer on how the pot works along with recipes for these sweet favorites and more. Armed with this knowledge, countertop cooking will become your go-to way for putting a brunch-time coffee cake or supper-time pots de crème on the table.

THE MODELS

The Instant Pot® is available in three sizes and in several models, each with different features and cooking programs. Each has slightly varying attributes, but all accomplish the same basic functions. The numbers in the model names, 50, 60, and 80, refer to the size of the pot, or 5, 6, and 8 quarts, respectively. If you're primarily cooking for four to six people, a model with a 6-quart capacity should be sufficient. The recipes in this book were developed in the Williams Sonoma Test Kitchen using the DUO60 Plus Instant Pot®. For best results, read all of the instructions that came with your Instant Pot® before you begin using it.

Instant Pot® Primer

Only two cooking programs are called for in this book, Pressure Cook (labeled Manual on some older models), which is equivalent to cooking in a pressure cooker, and Sauté, a non-pressure program that is used just once, to thicken a pudding. Here is how to use the Pressure Cook program:

- Put the food to be cooked into the pot as directed in individual recipes. In most cases, this involves either a steam rack with handles or a trivet (see page 10).

- Cover the pot with the lid, lock the lid in place, and turn the Steam Release handle (the valve) to Sealing.

- Press the Pressure Cook button and the digital display will light up. You now have 10 seconds to set the cook time indicated in the recipe using the - and + keys and to adjust the pressure level. All of the recipes in this book call for High pressure, which is the default setting.

- The pot will beep and the lighted display will indicate the cycle has started. At the end of the cycle, the pot will beep again and automatically end cooking.

- You can release the pressure in three different ways: natural, quick, or a combination. All the recipes in this book call for a natural release for a specified time, followed by a quick-release. When the display light goes off, carefully remove the lid.

HIGH ALTITUDE COOKING

If you are using the Pressure Cook program at 3,000 feet, you will need to increase cook times by 5 percent. For every 1,000 feet above 3,000 feet, increase cook times by an additional 5 percent: 10 percent at 4,000 feet, 15 percent at 5,000 feet, and so on.

Instant Pot® Tips for Desserts

Whether you're making a soup or a cheesecake, the basic rules of Instant Pot® cooking apply. Here are simple guidelines—both dessert specific and general—to review before you get started.

- Cut or form ingredients—from pieces of dough to slices of fruit—into similar-size pieces so they cook evenly. Level batters in their pans for even cakes.

- Grease cake pans thoroughly for easy unmolding. Nonstick cooking spray works better than butter, as the milk solids in butter can encourage sticking.

- Cover cake pans and ramekins with aluminum foil to prevent condensation from the steam created under pressure from dripping onto your dessert.

- Cook time starts from when the pot reaches full pressure, not from the moment when the button was pressed. Building up and releasing pressure can take from a few minutes to a half hour or more, depending on what's being cooked, its temperature, its volume, and the release method.

- Always wait until the float valve (pin) on the lid drops, indicating all the pressure has been released, before removing the lid.

- These tools are essential for preparing the recipes in this book: 6-cup Bundt pan, 7-inch springform pan, 4-ounce ceramic ramekins, ½-pint canning jars, trivet, and steam rack with handles. (If your pot model did not include a steam rack, you can use the trivet and a homemade sling for lowering and raising pans into and out of the pot: Place the trivet in the pot. Fold a 20-inch-long piece of aluminum foil in half lengthwise twice to create a 3-inch-wide sling, center the sling underneath the pan, and use the two ends as handles to lower the pan onto the trivet and to retrieve it after cooking.)

Salted Caramel Cheesecake with Pretzel Crumb Crust

Use your favorite salted caramel sauce—homemade or store-bought—for this easy cheesecake that pairs a salty-malty pretzel crumb crust with a sweet, creamy filling. If the sauce has hardened, warm just until fluid in the microwave.

To make the crust, lightly spray a 7-inch springform pan with nonstick cooking spray. In a small bowl, stir together the pretzel crumbs, brown sugar, and butter until a crumbly, evenly moistened mixture forms. Press the mixture evenly onto the bottom of the prepared pan, packing it tightly. Place the pan in the freezer while you make the filling, at least 15 minutes.

To make the filling, in a stand mixer fitted with the paddle attachment, beat the cream cheese on medium speed until smooth. Add the granulated sugar and beat until combined, stopping to scrape down the sides of the bowl. Add the sour cream, eggs, vanilla, and caramel sauce and continue to beat on medium speed until smooth and creamy, about 1 minute. Pour into the prepared pan and smooth the top. Cover the pan with a paper towel and then with aluminum foil, crimping the edges.

Pour the water into the Instant Pot®. Place the springform pan on the steam rack. Using the rack handles, lower the pan into the pot. Lock the lid in place and turn the valve to Sealing. Press the Pressure Cook button and set the cook time for 36 minutes at high pressure.

Let the steam release naturally for 15 minutes, then turn the valve to Venting to quick-release any residual steam. Remove the lid and transfer the springform pan to a cooling rack. Remove the foil and paper towel and let cool for 30 minutes. Cover with plastic wrap and refrigerate for at least 3 hours.

To serve, remove the pan sides and cut into wedges. Serve chilled, topped with a drizzle of sauce and a sprinkle of salt.

Serves 8

FOR THE CRUST

1 cup fine pretzel crumbs (about 4 oz whole pretzels)

2 tablespoons firmly packed light brown sugar

4 tablespoons unsalted butter, melted

FOR THE FILLING

2 packages (8 oz each) cream cheese, at room temperature

½ cup granulated sugar

¼ cup sour cream

2 large eggs, at room temperature

2 teaspoons vanilla extract

¼ cup salted caramel sauce

2 cups water

Salted caramel sauce, for drizzling

Flaky sea salt, for sprinkling

Omit the flaky salt and scatter a small handful of broken pretzels on top for both crunch and some extra malty-salty flavor.

Dress up each slice with a dollop of lightly sweetened whipped cream sprinkled with grated lemon zest or topped with a tiny sprig of fresh mint.

Lemon-Blueberry Cheesecake

This berry-topped cheesecake is equally delicious made with strawberry, blackberry, or raspberry preserves and berries. For an extra boost of lemon flavor, add 2 teaspoons grated lemon zest to the crust mixture.

To make the crust, lightly spray a 7-inch springform pan with nonstick cooking spray. In a small bowl, stir together the graham cracker crumbs, sugar, and butter until a crumbly, evenly moistened mixture forms. Press the mixture evenly onto the bottom of the prepared pan, packing it tightly. Freeze for at least 15 minutes.

To make the filling, in a stand mixer fitted with the paddle attachment, beat the cream cheese on medium speed until smooth. Add the sugar and beat until combined, stopping to scrape down the sides of the bowl as needed. Add the sour cream, eggs, vanilla, lemon juice and zest, and salt and continue to beat on medium speed until smooth and creamy, about 1 minute. Pour into the prepared pan and smooth the top. Cover the pan with a paper towel and then with aluminum foil, crimping the edges.

Pour the water into the Instant Pot®. Place the springform pan on the steam rack. Using the rack handles, lower the pan into the pot. Lock the lid in place and turn the valve to Sealing. Press the Pressure Cook button and set the cook time for 36 minutes at high pressure.

Let the steam release naturally for 15 minutes, then turn the valve to Venting to quick-release any residual steam. Carefully remove the lid and transfer the springform pan to a cooling rack. Uncover the cheesecake and let cool for 30 minutes. Cover and refrigerate for 2 hours.

To make the topping, in a saucepan over medium-low heat, simmer the preserves and lemon zest. Add the berries and simmer until they burst, about 2 minutes. Let cool for 5 minutes, then pour over the chilled cheesecake. Re-cover and chill for at least 1 hour or up to overnight, then remove the pan sides and serve.

Serves 8

FOR THE CRUST

1 cup fine graham cracker crumbs (about 9 whole crackers)

2 tablespoons sugar

3 tablespoons unsalted butter, melted

FOR THE FILLING

2 packages (8 oz each) cream cheese, at room temperature

¾ cup sugar

¼ cup sour cream

2 large eggs, at room temperature

2 teaspoons vanilla extract

3 tablespoons fresh lemon juice

2 teaspoons grated lemon zest

¼ teaspoon kosher salt

2 cups water

FOR THE TOPPING

½ cup blueberry preserves

1 teaspoon grated lemon zest

1 cup fresh blueberries

Classic Cheesecake

Here, a creamy filling and a sweet graham cracker crust equal the perfect New York cheesecake. To help shape the crust, spray the bottom of a small glass with nonstick cooking spray and use to press the crumbs firmly in place.

To make the crust, lightly spray a 7-inch springform pan with nonstick cooking spray. In a small bowl, stir together the graham cracker crumbs, sugar, and butter until a crumbly, evenly moistened mixture forms. Press the mixture evenly onto the bottom of the prepared pan, packing it tightly. Place the pan in the freezer while you make the filling, at least 15 minutes.

To make the filling, in a stand mixer fitted with the paddle attachment, beat the cream cheese on medium speed until smooth. Add the sugar and beat until combined, stopping to scrape down the sides of the bowl as needed. Add the sour cream, eggs, vanilla, lemon juice, and salt and continue to beat on medium speed until smooth and creamy, about 1 minute. Pour into the prepared pan and smooth the top. Cover the pan with a paper towel and then with aluminum foil, crimping the edges.

Pour the water into the Instant Pot®. Place the springform pan on the steam rack. Using the rack handles, lower the pan into the pot. Lock the lid in place and turn the valve to Sealing. Press the Pressure Cook button and set the cook time for 36 minutes at high pressure.

Let the steam release naturally for 15 minutes, then turn the valve to Venting to quick-release any residual steam. Carefully remove the lid and transfer the springform pan to a cooling rack. Remove the foil and paper towel and let the cheesecake cool for 30 minutes. Cover with plastic wrap and refrigerate for at least 3 hours or up to overnight.

To serve, remove the pan sides and cut into wedges. Serve chilled, topped with whipped cream.

Serves 8

FOR THE CRUST

1 cup graham cracker crumbs (9 whole crackers)

2 tablespoons granulated sugar

3 tablespoons unsalted butter, melted

FOR THE FILLING

2 packages (8 oz each) cream cheese, at room temperature

¾ cup granulated sugar

¼ sour cream

2 eggs, room temperature

2 teaspoons vanilla extract

2 teaspoons lemon juice

¼ teaspoon kosher salt

2 cups water

Whipped cream, for serving

Classic Rice Pudding

In this easy Instant Pot® take on old-fashioned stove-top rice pudding, you skip the long stirring but not the silky, thick texture and rich, creamy flavor. To add a citrusy note, stir in 1 teaspoon grated lemon zest with the vanilla.

Combine the rice, cinnamon stick, salt, and water in the Instant Pot®. Lock the lid in place and turn the valve to Sealing. Press the Pressure Cook button and set the cook time for 3 minutes at high pressure.

While the rice is cooking, in a small bowl, stir together the sugar and ground cinnamon. In a medium bowl, whisk the eggs until blended, then whisk in the cinnamon-sugar, milk, vanilla, and raisins, mixing well.

Let the steam release naturally for 10 minutes, then turn the valve to Venting to quick-release any residual steam. Carefully remove the lid and discard the cinnamon stick.

Press the Cancel button to reset the program, then select the Sauté button. Pour the milk mixture into the cooked rice and stir to mix. Bring just to a simmer and cook, stirring occasionally, until slightly thickened, about 2 minutes. Press the Cancel button to turn off the pot, then stir in the butter. Serve right away.

Serves 6

1 cup Arborio rice

1 cinnamon stick

1 teaspoon kosher salt

1½ cups water

½ cup sugar

1 teaspoon ground cinnamon

2 large eggs

2 cups whole milk

1 teaspoon vanilla paste or vanilla extract

½ cup raisins

1 teaspoon unsalted butter

Molten Chocolate Cakes

To serve these decadent cakes unmolded, invert a plate over each ramekin, flip the plate and ramekin together, and then give the ramekin a tap to release the cake onto the plate. Add a few raspberries to each plate along with the cream.

Lightly spray five 4-oz ramekins with nonstick cooking spray, then dust with sugar. Combine the butter and chocolate in a heatproof bowl, place over (not touching) simmering water in a saucepan, and heat, stirring occasionally, until melted and smooth. Remove from the heat, whisk in the sugar until dissolved, and then whisk in the whole eggs, egg yolks, and vanilla. Sift the cocoa powder, flour, and salt over the chocolate mixture, then fold in gently until no dry streaks remain. Divide evenly among the prepared ramekins. Cover each ramekin with aluminum foil, crimping the edges.

Pour the water into the Instant Pot® and insert the steam rack. If using an 8-quart Instant Pot®, place the ramekins in a single layer on the rack. If using a 6-quart Instant Pot®, place 4 ramekins on the rack and stack the fifth one on top in the center. Lock the lid in place and turn the valve to Sealing. Press the Pressure Cook button and set the cook time for 10 minutes at high pressure.

Let the steam release naturally for 5 minutes, then turn the valve to Venting to quick-release any residual steam. Carefully remove the lid and transfer the cakes to a cooling rack. Remove the foil and let cool for 5 minutes.

Serve warm plated or in the ramekins, topped with whipped cream.

Serves 5

½ cup unsalted butter

1 cup semisweet chocolate chips (6 oz)

⅔ cup sugar

2 large whole eggs plus 2 large yolks

2 teaspoons vanilla extract

3 tablespoons Dutch-process cocoa powder

3 tablespoons all-purpose flour

¼ teaspoon kosher salt

2 cups water

Whipped cream, for serving

Using a block of semisweet chocolate and a vegetable peeler or the large holes on a box grater-shredder, make small shards of chocolate for dusting each serving.

Carrot Cake with Cream Cheese Frosting

A perennial birthday favorite, carrot cake turns out wonderfully dense and moist when cooked in the Instant Pot®. If you're pressed for time, skip the frosting and serve the cake as a single layer, dusting the top with confectioners' sugar.

To make the cake, lightly spray a 7-inch springform pan with nonstick cooking spray. In a bowl, whisk together the flour, cinnamon, nutmeg, allspice, salt, baking soda, and baking powder. In another bowl, whisk together the eggs, both sugars, oil, and vanilla until smooth. Fold half of the flour mixture into the egg mixture until well mixed, then fold in the remaining flour mixture just until no dry streaks remain. Finally, fold in the carrots and currants. Transfer to the prepared pan and smooth the top. Cover the pan with aluminum foil, crimping the edges.

Pour the water into the Instant Pot®. Place the springform pan on the steam rack and lower the pan into the pot. Lock the lid in place and turn the valve to Sealing. Press the Pressure Cook button and set the cook time for 65 minutes at high pressure.

Let the steam release naturally for 15 minutes, then turn the valve to Venting to quick-release any residual steam. Carefully remove the lid and transfer the springform pan to a cooling rack. Remove the foil and let the cake cool in the pan for 15 minutes, then remove the pan sides and let cool completely.

Meanwhile, make the frosting. In a bowl, using an electric mixer, beat together the cream cheese and butter on medium-high speed until smooth, about 45 seconds. Beat in the sour cream, vanilla, and salt until well mixed. On low speed, beat in the confectioners' sugar until combined, then increase the speed to medium-high and beat until smooth and fluffy, about 1 minute.

Split the cake into 2 layers. Spread a thin layer of frosting on the bottom layer, top with the second layer, and then frost the top and sides. Cut into wedges to serve.

Serves 8

FOR THE CAKE

1 ¼ cups all-purpose flour

1 teaspoon ground cinnamon

½ teaspoon ground nutmeg

¼ teaspoon ground allspice

1 teaspoon kosher salt

½ teaspoon baking soda

½ teaspoon baking powder

2 large eggs

¾ cup granulated sugar

¼ cup firmly packed dark brown sugar

¾ cup canola oil

1 teaspoon vanilla extract

6 oz carrots, peeled and grated (about 1 ½ cups)

¼ cup dried currants

2 cups water

FOR THE FROSTING

1 package (8 oz) cream cheese, at room temperature

4 tablespoons unsalted butter, at room temperature

2 tablespoons sour cream

1 teaspoon vanilla extract

¼ teaspoon kosher salt

¾ cup confectioners' sugar

Chocolate Espresso Bundt Cake

Coffee and chocolate lovers alike will line up for this tender, moist cake. For a stronger espresso flavor, increase the espresso powder to 2 tablespoons. Pair each slice with a scoop of ice cream drizzled with Hot Fudge Sauce (page 49).

Spray a 6-cup Bundt pan with nonstick cooking spray. In a bowl, whisk together the flour, cocoa powder, baking powder, baking soda, and salt. In a small bowl, whisk the espresso powder into the hot water until dissolved.

In a large bowl, whisk together the butter, sugar, egg, and vanilla until smooth, then whisk in the espresso mixture. Add the flour mixture to the butter mixture in two batches alternately with the buttermilk, beginning and ending with the flour mixture and stirring just until mixed after each addition. Transfer to the prepared pan and smooth the top. Cover the pan with aluminum foil, crimping the edges.

Pour the water into the Instant Pot®. Place the Bundt pan on the steam rack. Using the rack handles, lower the pan into the pot. Lock the lid in place and turn the valve to Sealing. Press the Pressure Cook button and set the cook time for 50 minutes at high pressure.

Let the steam release naturally for 15 minutes, then turn the valve to Venting to quick-release any residual steam. Carefully remove the lid and transfer the Bundt pan to a cooling rack. Remove the foil and let the cake cool in the pan for 10 minutes, then invert the pan onto a serving plate, lift off the pan, and let the cake cool for 10 minutes longer.

Using a fine-mesh sieve, dust the top of the cake with cocoa powder. Slice into wedges and serve warm or at room temperature. Store any leftovers in an airtight container at room temperature for up to 3 days.

Serves 6-8

1 cup all-purpose flour

½ cup Dutch-process cocoa powder, plus more for dusting

2 teaspoons baking powder

¼ teaspoon baking soda

½ teaspoon kosher salt

1 tablespoon espresso powder

1 tablespoon hot water

½ cup unsalted butter, melted and cooled

¾ cup sugar

1 large egg

2 teaspoons vanilla extract

½ cup buttermilk

1½ cups water

Vanilla Bean Bundt Cake with Vanilla Glaze

An ideal teatime treat, this vanilla-infused Bundt cake will keep in an airtight container at room temperature for up to 3 days. For a special occasion, serve each slice with a scoop of French vanilla ice cream.

To make the cake, spray a 6-cup Bundt pan with nonstick cooking spray. In a bowl, whisk together the flour, baking powder, baking soda, and salt. In a large bowl, whisk together the butter, sugar, egg, and vanilla until smooth. Add the flour mixture to the butter mixture in two batches alternately with the buttermilk, beginning and ending with the flour mixture and stirring just until mixed after each addition. Transfer to the prepared pan and smooth the top. Cover the pan with aluminum foil, crimping the edges.

Pour the water into the Instant Pot®. Place the Bundt pan on the steam rack. Using the rack handles, lower the pan into the pot. Lock the lid in place and turn the valve to Sealing. Press the Pressure Cook button and set the cook time for 50 minutes at high pressure.

Let the steam release naturally for 15 minutes, then turn the valve to Venting to quick-release any residual steam. Carefully remove the lid and transfer the Bundt pan to a cooling rack. Remove the foil and let the cake cool in the pan for 10 minutes, then invert the pan onto a serving plate, lift off the pan, and let cool for 10 minutes longer.

Meanwhile, make the glaze. In a small bowl, whisk together the confectioners' sugar, 3 tablespoons of the cream, and the vanilla until smooth. For a thinner glaze, whisk in the remaining 1 tablespoon cream.

Pour the glaze over the slightly warm cake. Slice into wedges and serve warm or at room temperature.

Serves 6–8

FOR THE CAKE

1½ cups all-purpose flour

2 teaspoons baking powder

¼ teaspoon baking soda

½ teaspoon salt

½ cup unsalted butter, melted and cooled

¾ cup sugar

1 large egg

2 tablespoons vanilla paste or vanilla extract, or seeds from 1 vanilla bean

½ cup buttermilk

1½ cups water

FOR THE GLAZE

½ cup confectioners' sugar

3–4 tablespoons heavy cream

½ teaspoon vanilla paste or vanilla extract, or seeds from ¼ vanilla bean

Lemon–Poppy Seed Bundt Cake with Lemon Glaze

Moist and irresistible, this lemony cake, dotted with nutty-tasting poppy seeds, tastes even better dressed up with a dollop of Lemon Curd (page 45). To prevent sticking, make sure to grease every ridge, crevice, and bump of the pan.

To make the cake, spray a 6-cup Bundt pan with nonstick cooking spray. In a medium bowl, whisk together the flour, baking powder, baking soda, salt, and poppyseeds. In a large bowl, whisk together the butter, sugar, egg, lemon juice and zest, and vanilla until smooth. Add the flour mixture to the butter mixture in two batches alternately with the buttermilk, beginning and ending with the flour mixture and stirring just until mixed after each addition. Transfer the batter to the prepared pan and smooth the top. Cover the pan with foil, crimping the edges.

Pour the water into the Instant Pot®. Place the Bundt pan on the steam rack. Using the rack handles, lower the pan into the pot. Lock the lid in place and turn the valve to Sealing. Press the Pressure Cook button and set the cook time for 50 minutes at high pressure.

Let the steam release naturally for 15 minutes, then turn the valve to Venting to quick-release any residual steam. Remove the lid and transfer the Bundt pan to a cooling rack. Remove the foil and let the cake cool in the pan for 10 minutes, then invert the pan onto a serving plate, lift off the pan, and let cool for 10 minutes longer.

Meanwhile, make the glaze. In a small bowl, whisk together the confectioners' sugar, lemon juice and zest, and vanilla until smooth.

Pour the glaze over the slightly warm cake. Slice into wedges and serve warm or at room temperature. Store any leftovers in an airtight container at room temperature for up to 3 days.

Serves 6-8

FOR THE CAKE

1½ cups all-purpose flour

2 teaspoons baking powder

¼ teaspoon baking soda

½ teaspoon kosher salt

1 tablespoon poppy seeds

½ cup unsalted butter, melted and cooled

¾ cup sugar

1 large egg

3 tablespoons fresh lemon juice

1 tablespoon grated lemon zest

2 teaspoons vanilla extract

½ cup buttermilk

1½ cups water

FOR THE GLAZE

½ cup confectioners' sugar

3 tablespoons fresh lemon juice

1 teaspoon grated lemon zest

½ teaspoon pure vanilla extract

Add a few fresh berries—
blackberries, blueberries,
raspberries—or thin, ripe
pear slices to each serving.

Cardamom Coffee Cake

Cardamom brings a sweet, slightly piney, delicate flavor to this easy-to-like brunch cake. To give it a bright citrusy note, add 1 teaspoon grated orange zest to the filling and 1 tablespoon grated orange zest to the cake batter.

To make the filling, in a small bowl, stir together the brown sugar, cinnamon, cardamom, and salt.

To make the topping, in a small bowl, stir together the flour, brown sugar, cinnamon, and cardamom. Stir in the butter until a crumbly, evenly moistened mixture forms.

To make the cake, spray a 7-inch springform pan with nonstick cooking spray. In a bowl, whisk together the flour, baking powder, baking soda, and salt. In a large bowl, whisk together the butter, sugar, egg, and vanilla until smooth. Add the flour mixture to the butter mixture in two batches alternately with the milk, beginning and ending with the flour mixture and stirring just until mixed after each addition. Transfer half of the batter to the prepared pan and spread into an even layer. It will be thick and difficult to spread. Sprinkle evenly with the filling mixture, then top with the remaining batter, again spreading it evenly. Sprinkle the topping evenly over the surface. Cover the pan with aluminum foil, crimping the edges.

Pour the water into the Instant Pot®. Place the springform pan on the steam rack. Using the rack handles, lower the pan into the pot. Lock the lid in place and turn the valve to Sealing. Press the Pressure Cook button and set the cook time for 65 minutes at high pressure.

Let the steam release naturally for 10 minutes, then turn the valve to Venting to quick-release any residual steam. Carefully remove the lid and transfer the springform pan to a cooling rack. Remove the foil and let the cake cool for 10 minutes.

To serve, remove the pan sides, cut into wedges, and serve warm.

Serves 8

FOR THE FILLING

3 tablespoons firmly packed light brown sugar

1 1/2 teaspoons ground cinnamon

1/2 teaspoon ground cardamom

1/4 teaspoon kosher salt

FOR THE TOPPING

1/4 cup plus 1 tablespoon all-purpose flour

1/4 cup firmly packed light brown sugar

1/2 teaspoon ground cinnamon

1/4 teaspoon ground cardamom

2 tablespoons unsalted butter, melted

FOR THE CAKE

2 cups all-purpose flour

2 teaspoons baking powder

1/2 teaspoon baking soda

1 teaspoon kosher salt

1/2 cup unsalted butter, melted and cooled

1/2 cup granulated sugar

1 large egg

1 teaspoon vanilla extract

2/3 cup whole milk

1 1/2 cups water

White Chocolate Bread Pudding

For the best result, use the highest-quality white chocolate your budget allows. Other warm spices—nutmeg, cardamom, ginger—can be used in place of the cinnamon. If you opt to skip the sauce, add a spoonful of berries to each serving.

Lightly spray a 7-inch cake pan with nonstick cooking spray. In a saucepan over medium heat, combine the milk, vanilla, cinnamon, and salt and bring to a simmer. Meanwhile, in another bowl, whisk the egg yolks until blended, then whisk in the sugar, mixing well. When the milk mixture is at a simmer, remove the pan from the heat and whisk in the chocolate until melted and smooth. Slowly pour about ¼ cup of the hot milk mixture into the egg yolk mixture while whisking constantly. Then slowly pour the egg yolk–milk mixture back into the saucepan, again whisking constantly.

Put the croissants into a large bowl, pour in the warm milk mixture, and mix gently until evenly moistened. Transfer the mixture to the prepared pan, adding the last few pieces by hand to avoid spilling any liquid. Pour any liquid remaining in the bowl into the pan. Cover with aluminum foil, crimping the edges.

Pour the water into the Instant Pot®. Place the cake pan on the steam rack and lower the pan into the pot. Lock the lid in place and turn the valve to Sealing. Press the Pressure Cook button and set the cook time for 30 minutes at high pressure.

Turn the valve to Venting to quick-release the steam. Carefully remove the lid and transfer the cake pan to a cooling rack. Let the pudding cool for 5 minutes, then remove the foil.

Meanwhile, make the sauce, if using. In a small saucepan over medium heat, whisk together the cream, vanilla, and salt and bring to a simmer. Remove from the heat and whisk in the chocolate until melted and smooth.

To serve, cut into wedges and serve warm. Top each serving with the warm sauce, if using.

Serves 8–10

2 cups whole milk

2 tablespoons vanilla paste or vanilla extract

1 teaspoon ground cinnamon

1 ½ teaspoons kosher salt

2 large egg yolks

⅓ cup sugar

12 oz white chocolate, coarsely chopped

1 lb day-old croissants (4–5 croissants), ripped into 1-inch pieces

1 ½ cups water

FOR THE SAUCE (OPTIONAL)

½ cup heavy cream

1 tablespoon vanilla paste or vanilla extract

½ teaspoon kosher salt

2 oz white chocolate, coarsely chopped

Coat the Bundt pan well with cooking spray, or the sugar-coated biscuit pieces will stick to its flutes and ridges.

Cinnamon-Sugar Monkey Bread

A Bundt pan gives this popular, pull-apart breakfast or brunch bread a special-occasion look. To add a bit of crunch, as you pour the butter-and-spice-coated biscuits into the pan, sprinkle ⅓ cup chopped pecans in among the pieces.

To make the bread, spray a 6-cup Bundt pan with nonstick cooking spray. In a bowl, combine the butter and ½ teaspoon of the salt. Using the tip of a knife, scrape the seeds from the vanilla bean into the bowl, then stir to mix well. In a second bowl, stir together the cinnamon, granulated and brown sugars, and the remaining ½ teaspoon salt.

Put the biscuit pieces into the melted butter mixture and toss until the dough is evenly coated. Pour the butter-coated biscuit pieces into the cinnamon-sugar mixture and toss until evenly coated. Pour the biscuit mixture into the prepared pan. Cover the pan with aluminum foil, crimping the edges.

Pour the water into the Instant Pot®. Place the Bundt pan on the steam rack. Using the rack handles, lower the pan into the pot. Lock the lid in place and turn the valve to Sealing. Press the Pressure Cook button and set the cook time for 21 minutes at high pressure.

Let the steam release for 15 minutes, then turn the valve to Venting to quick-release any residual steam. Carefully remove the lid and transfer the Bundt pan to a cooling rack. Remove the foil and let the bread cool in the pan for about 10 minutes, then invert the pan onto a serving plate and lift off the pan.

To make the glaze, in a small bowl, whisk together the confectioners' sugar, milk, vanilla, and salt until smooth.

Pour the glaze over the warm bread and serve warm.

Serves 8-10

FOR THE BREAD

¾ cup unsalted butter, melted and cooled

1 teaspoon kosher salt

1 vanilla bean, split lengthwise

1 tablespoon ground cinnamon

½ cup granulated sugar

½ cup firmly packed light brown sugar

1 package (1 lb) refrigerated biscuit dough, each biscuit quartered

1½ cups water

FOR THE GLAZE

¼ cup confectioners' sugar

1½ teaspoons whole milk

¼ teaspoon vanilla extract

Pinch of kosher salt

Key Lime Pie

For the best flavor and the most juice, look for plump, firm Key limes with smooth, greenish-yellow skin and a floral citrusy aroma. In a pinch, bottled Key lime juice and zest from conventional limes can be substituted.

To make the crust, lightly spray a 7-inch springform pan with nonstick cooking spray. In a bowl, stir together the graham cracker crumbs, sugar, and butter until a crumbly, evenly moistened mixture forms. Press the mixture evenly onto the bottom of the prepared pan, packing it tightly. Place the pan in the freezer while you make the filling, at least 15 minutes.

To make the filling, in a bowl, whisk together the egg yolks and condensed milk, mixing well. Whisk in the lime juice, sour cream, and lime zest until incorporated. Pour into the prepared pan. Cover the pan with a paper towel and then with aluminum foil, crimping the edges.

Pour the water into the Instant Pot®. Place the springform pan on the steam rack. Using the rack handles, lower the pan into the pot. Lock the lid in place and turn the valve to Sealing. Press the Pressure Cook button and set the cook time for 20 minutes at high pressure.

Let the steam release naturally for 10 minutes, then turn the valve to Venting to quick-release any residual steam. Remove the lid and transfer the springform pan to a cooling rack. Remove the foil and paper towel, let the pie cool in the pan for about 5 minutes, then remove the pan sides and let cool to room temperature. Wrap with plastic wrap and refrigerate for at least 1 hour or up to overnight before serving.

Just before serving, in a bowl, using a handheld mixer, beat together the cream, confectioners' sugar, and vanilla on medium speed until soft peaks form. Spread the whipped cream on top of the pie, then garnish with the lime zest. Cut into wedges and serve chilled.

Serves 6–8

FOR THE CRUST

1 cup fine graham cracker crumbs (about 9 whole crackers)

2 tablespoons granulated sugar

3 tablespoons unsalted butter, melted

FOR THE FILLING

4 large egg yolks

1 can (14 oz) sweetened condensed milk

½ cup fresh Key lime juice

⅓ cup sour cream

2 tablespoons grated Key lime zest

1½ cups water

FOR THE TOPPING

1 cup heavy cream

¼ cup confectioners' sugar

1 teaspoon vanilla extract

Grated Key lime zest, for sprinkling

Chocolate Chip Banana Bread

You can switch up the flavors here, substituting butterscotch chips for the semisweet chocolate chips or using half butterscotch and half chocolate. Any leftover bread will keep in an airtight container at room temperature for up to 2 days.

Lightly spray a 7-inch springform pan with nonstick cooking spray. In a stand mixer fitted with the paddle attachment, beat together the butter and sugars on medium speed until smooth and light. On low speed, add the eggs and vanilla and beat until incorporated, then beat in the bananas and buttermilk until blended.

In a bowl, whisk together the flour, baking soda, baking powder, cinnamon, and salt. With the mixer on low speed, gradually pour the flour mixture into the butter mixture, beating just until fully incorporated. Fold in the chocolate chips. Transfer to the prepared pan and smooth the top. Cover the pan with aluminum foil, crimping the edges.

Pour the water into the Instant Pot®. Place the springform pan on the steam rack. Using the rack handles, lower the pan into the pot. Lock the lid in place and turn the valve to Sealing. Press the Pressure Cook button and set the cook time for 55 minutes at high pressure.

Let the steam release naturally for 15 minutes, then turn the valve to Venting to quick-release any residual steam. Carefully remove the lid and transfer the springform pan to a cooling rack. Remove the foil and let the bread cool in the pan for about 5 minutes.

To serve, remove the pan sides and serve warm or at room temperature.

Serves 8–10

½ cup unsalted butter, at room temperature

¾ cup firmly packed light brown sugar

¼ cup granulated sugar

2 large eggs, whisked

2 teaspoons vanilla paste or vanilla extract

3 ripe bananas, peeled and mashed

¼ cup buttermilk

2 cups all-purpose flour

1 teaspoon baking soda

1 teaspoon baking powder

1 teaspoon ground cinnamon

1½ teaspoons salt

½ cup semisweet chocolate chips

1½ cups water

Maple-Walnut Banana Bread

If your bananas aren't ripe, tuck them into a paper bag, add an apple, and close the top loosely. This combo increases the production of ethylene gas—the invisible gas that promotes ripening—so your bananas will be ready in a day or two.

Lightly spray a 6-inch springform pan with nonstick cooking spray. In a stand mixer fitted with the paddle attachment, beat together the butter and sugar on medium speed until smooth and light. On low speed, add the eggs and vanilla and beat until incorporated. Then beat in ¼ cup of the maple syrup, the bananas, and buttermilk until blended.

In a bowl, whisk together the flour, baking soda, baking powder, cinnamon, and salt. With the mixer on low speed, gradually pour the flour mixture into the butter mixture, beating just until fully incorporated. Fold in the walnuts. Transfer to the prepared pan and smooth the top. Cover the pan with aluminum foil, crimping the edges.

Pour the water into the Instant Pot®. Place the springform pan on the steam rack. Using the rack handles, lower the pan into the pot. Lock the lid in place and turn the valve to Sealing. Press the Pressure Cook button and set the cook time for 55 minutes at high pressure.

Let the steam release naturally for 15 minutes, then turn the valve to Venting to quick-release any residual steam. Carefully remove the lid and transfer the springform pan to a cooling rack. Remove the foil and let the bread cool in the pan for about 5 minutes.

To serve, remove the pan sides and brush the remaining ¼ cup maple syrup on the warm bread. Serve warm or at room temperature.

Serves 8-10

½ cup unsalted butter, at room temperature

½ cup firmly packed light brown sugar

2 large eggs, whisked

2 teaspoons vanilla paste or vanilla extract

½ cup maple syrup

3 ripe bananas, peeled and mashed

¼ cup buttermilk

2 cups all-purpose flour

1 teaspoon baking soda

1 teaspoon baking powder

1 teaspoon ground cinnamon

2 teaspoons kosher salt

¾ cup chopped walnuts

1½ cups water

Chocolate-Hazelnut Pots de Crème

You can serve these luscious French-inspired custards just as they are, but a dollop of whipped cream or crème fraîche and a few berries or a dusting of grated chocolate dresses them up nicely for company.

In a saucepan over low heat, combine the milk, sugar, and salt and bring to a simmer, stirring to dissolve the sugar. Meanwhile, in a heatproof bowl, whisk the egg yolks until blended.

When the milk mixture is at a simmer, remove from the heat and whisk in the chocolate chips and Nutella until melted and smooth. Slowly pour about ¼ cup of the hot milk mixture into the egg yolks while whisking constantly. Then slowly pour the egg yolk–milk mixture back into the saucepan, again whisking constantly.

Pour the custard through a fine-mesh sieve set over a large pitcher. Divide the custard evenly among six 4-oz ramekins. Cover each ramekin with aluminum foil, crimping the edges.

Pour the water into the Instant Pot® and put the steam rack into the pot with the handles up. Place 3 ramekins on the rack, making sure they are level. Lock the lid in place and turn the valve to Sealing. Press the Pressure Cook button and set the cook time for 6 minutes at high pressure.

Let the steam release naturally for 15 minutes, then turn the valve to Venting to quick-release any residual steam. Carefully remove the lid and transfer the ramekins to a cooling rack. Let cool for about 5 minutes before removing the foil. Repeat to cook the remaining 3 ramekins.

Let the ramekins cool to room temperature, cover with plastic wrap, and refrigerate for at least 4 hours or up to overnight before serving. Serve chilled.

Serves 6

2 cups whole milk

⅓ cup sugar

1 teaspoon kosher salt

5 large egg yolks

⅔ cup semisweet chocolate chips

1 cup Nutella or hazelnut butter

1½ cups water

Salted Caramel Pots de Crème

These *pots de crème* are all about caramel, so if you opt to purchase the caramel sauce rather than make your own, look for one that lists only a few ingredients—butter, cream, sugar, and natural flavors—for the best result.

In a saucepan over low heat, combine the milk, sugar, and kosher salt and bring to a simmer, stirring to dissolve the sugar. Meanwhile, in a heatproof bowl, whisk the egg yolks until blended. Pour the caramel sauce into a second heatproof bowl.

When the milk mixture is at a simmer, remove from the heat, pour over the caramel sauce, and whisk until the sauce melts and is fully incorporated. Slowly pour about ¼ cup of the hot caramel-milk mixture into the egg yolks while whisking constantly. Then slowly pour the egg yolk–milk mixture back into the saucepan, again whisking constantly.

Pour the custard through a fine-mesh sieve set over a large pitcher. Divide the custard evenly among six 4-oz ramekins. Cover each ramekin with aluminum foil, crimping the edges.

Pour the water into the Instant Pot® and put the steam rack into the pot with the handles up. Place 3 ramekins on the rack, making sure they are level. Lock the lid in place and turn the valve to Sealing. Press the Pressure Cook button and set the cook time for 6 minutes at high pressure.

Let the steam release naturally for 15 minutes, then turn the valve to Venting to quick-release any residual steam. Carefully remove the lid and transfer the ramekins to a cooling rack. Let cool for about 5 minutes before removing the foil. Repeat to cook the remaining 3 ramekins.

Let cool to room temperature, cover with plastic wrap, and refrigerate for at least 4 hours or up to overnight before serving. Top each ramekin with a pinch of sea salt and chopped nuts, if using, and serve chilled.

2 cups whole milk

⅓ cup sugar

1 teaspoon kosher salt

5 large egg yolks

1 cup caramel sauce

1½ cups water

Flaky sea salt, for garnish

Chopped nuts, for garnish (optional)

Serves 6

To cook all 6 custards at once, arrange 3 ramekins on the steam rack, place a heatproof plate on top of the ramekins, and then set the remaining 3 ramekins on top of the plate.

Sticky Toffee Pudding

Cooks in Britain and Canada argue over which country originated this rich, gooey, crowd-pleasing dessert. Forgot to soak the dates overnight? No problem. Bring them to a boil in water to cover, let stand for 15 minutes, then drain.

Spray a 7-inch springform pan with nonstick cooking spray. In a bowl, whisk together the flour, baking powder, baking soda, salt, cinnamon, cloves, and nutmeg. In a food processor, process the dates to a smooth paste, about 2 minutes.

In a stand mixer fitted with the paddle attachment, beat the butter on medium speed until smooth and creamy, then add the sugar and beat until light and fluffy, about 2 minutes. Add the egg and vanilla and beat until thoroughly mixed, then beat in the puréed dates. On low speed, add the flour mixture and beat just until combined. Pour into the prepared pan and smooth the top. Cover with aluminum foil, crimping the edges.

Pour the water into the Instant Pot®. Place the springform pan on the steam rack. Using the rack handles, lower the pan into the pot. Lock the lid in place and turn the valve to Sealing. Press the Pressure Cook button and set the cook time for 50 minutes at high pressure.

Let the steam release naturally for 10 minutes, then turn the valve to Venting to quick-release any residual steam. Carefully remove the lid, transfer the springform pan to a cooling rack, and let cool for 5 minutes.

Meanwhile, make the caramel sauce. In a small saucepan over medium heat, melt the butter. Whisk in the sugar, cream, vanilla, and salt and bring to a simmer. Cook, whisking constantly, until slightly thickened and the color darkens, about 5 minutes. When the sauce is ready, uncover the cake and, using a fork, pierce it about eight times to create tiny holes all over the top. Pour the caramel sauce evenly over the cake and let stand for 10 minutes. Remove the pan sides, cut into wedges, and serve warm.

Serves 8–10

¾ cup all-purpose flour

1¼ teaspoons baking powder

½ teaspoon baking soda

1 teaspoon kosher salt

½ teaspoon ground cinnamon

¼ teaspoon ground cloves

⅛ teaspoon ground nutmeg

1½ cups pitted dates (6 oz), soaked overnight in water to cover and drained

4 tablespoons unsalted butter, at room temperature

¾ cup firmly packed dark brown sugar

1 large egg

1 teaspoon vanilla extract

1½ cups water

FOR THE CARAMEL SAUCE

6 tablespoons unsalted butter

¾ cup firmly packed dark brown sugar

½ cup heavy cream

1 tablespoon vanilla extract

½ teaspoon kosher salt

Apple Crisp with Vanilla Ice Cream

Use a mix of tart—Granny Smith, Cortland, Jonathan—and sweet—Rome Beauty, Fuji, Gala—apples for this easy autumn dessert. For an extra touch of sweetness, drizzle each serving with a spoonful or two of warm Dulce de Leche (page 46).

To make the filling, combine the apples, lemon juice, cinnamon, nutmeg, allspice, water, sugar, and vanilla in the Instant Pot® and stir and toss to mix well.

To make the topping, in a bowl, stir together the butter, oats, flour, sugar, salt, and cinnamon until a stiff, coarse mixture forms. Sprinkle spoonfuls of the topping evenly over apples.

Lock the lid in place and turn the valve to Sealing. Press the Pressure Cook button and set the cook time for 8 minutes at high pressure.

Let the steam release naturally for 3 minutes, then turn the valve to Venting to quick-release any residual steam. Carefully remove the lid.

To serve, scoop the warm crisp into individual bowls and top each serving with a scoop of ice cream.

Serves 4

FOR THE FILLING

4 apples (about 2 lb), peeled, cored, and cut into 1-inch cubes

2 teaspoons fresh lemon juice

2 ½ teaspoons ground cinnamon

¾ teaspoon ground nutmeg

¾ teaspoon ground allspice

¼ cup water

¼ cup firmly packed light brown sugar

1 teaspoon vanilla extract

FOR THE TOPPING

4 tablespoons unsalted butter, melted

¾ cup old-fashioned rolled oats

¼ cup all-purpose flour

¼ cup firmly packed light brown sugar

½ teaspoon kosher salt

½ teaspoon ground cinnamon

Vanilla ice cream, for serving

Brown Sugar Peach Crisp

A warm, homemade stone-fruit crisp is a welcome sight on any summertime menu. You can trade out the yellow peaches for yellow nectarines and the vanilla ice cream for whipped crème fraîche or whipped cream.

To make the filling, in a bowl, combine the peaches, sugar, flour, cornstarch, lemon juice, vanilla, salt, and butter and stir and toss to coat the peaches evenly. Divide the peaches evenly among four 4-oz ramekins.

To make the topping, in a bowl, stir together butter, oats, flour, sugar, salt, cinnamon, and almonds until a coarse, crumbly mixture forms. Top each ramekin with one-fourth of the topping, spreading it evenly.

Pour the water into the Instant Pot® and insert the steam rack. Place the ramekins on the rack in a single layer. Lock the lid in place and turn the valve to Sealing. Press the Pressure Cook button and set the cook time for 25 minutes at high pressure.

Let the steam release naturally for 5 minutes, then turn the valve to Venting to quick-release any residual steam. Carefully remove the lid and remove the ramekins from the pot.

Serve the crisp warm, topping each ramekin with a scoop of ice cream.

Serves 4

FOR THE PEACHES

2 yellow peaches, halved, pitted, and sliced ½ inch thick

⅓ cup dark brown sugar

1 teaspoon all-purpose flour

1 teaspoon cornstarch

½ teaspoon fresh lemon juice

½ teaspoon vanilla extract

¼ teaspoon kosher salt

1 tablespoon unsalted butter, melted

FOR THE TOPPING

2 tablespoons unsalted butter, melted

⅓ cup old fashioned rolled oats

3 tablespoons all-purpose flour

2 tablespoons firmly packed dark brown sugar

½ teaspoon kosher salt

½ teaspoon ground cinnamon

3 tablespoons slivered blanched almonds

2 cups water

Vanilla ice cream, for serving

Lemon Curd

If you prefer a perfectly smooth lemon curd, after uncovering the jars and stirring the curd, pass it through a fine-mesh sieve. Enjoy this sweet-tart curd with fresh berries, scones or biscuits, or as a filling for layer cakes or tartlets.

In a large bowl, whisk together the whole eggs and egg yolks until blended and smooth. Add the sugar, lemon juice and zest, and butter and whisk until the sugar dissolves. Divide the lemon mixture evenly among four ½-pint canning jars. Screw on the lids.

Pour the water into the Instant Pot® and put the trivet into the pot. Put the jars on the trivet. Lock the lid in place and turn the valve to Sealing. Press the Pressure Cook button and set the cook time for 5 minutes at high pressure.

Let the steam release naturally for 10 minutes, then turn the valve to Venting to quick-release any residual steam. Carefully remove the lid, transfer the jars to a cooling rack, and let cool for 5 minutes.

Remove the jar lids and give the curd a stir. It will look chunky at first but will smooth out as you continue to stir. Serve warm or chilled. To store, re-cover the jars and refrigerate for up to 7 days.

Makes 4 half-pints

3 large whole eggs

3 large egg yolks

1 cup sugar

1 cup fresh lemon juice

1 tablespoon grated lemon zest

3 tablespoons unsalted butter, melted

1 cup water

Dulce de Leche

Boasting a creamy texture and complex flavor, this Latin American caramel sauce is delicious served over ice cream or yogurt, as a filling for sandwich cookies, folded inside crepes, used as a dip for fresh fruit, or stirred into hot coffee or a milk shake.

In a large bowl (preferably with a spout), combine the condensed milk and vanilla and stir until the vanilla is evenly distributed. Divide evenly among four ½-pint canning jars. Screw on the lids.

Pour the water into the Instant Pot® and put the trivet into the pot. Put the jars on the trivet. Lock the lid in place and turn the valve to Sealing. Press the Pressure Cook button and set the cook time for 40 minutes at high pressure.

Let the steam release naturally for 10 minutes, then turn the valve to Venting to quick-release any residual steam. Carefully remove the lid, transfer the jars to a cooling rack, and let cool for 5 minutes.

Remove the lids and use warm or at room temperature. To store, re-cover the jars and refrigerate for up to 2 weeks. To return the sauce to a pourable consistency, reheat gently in a double boiler or microwave.

Makes 4 half-pints

3 cans (14 oz each) sweetened condensed milk

1 tablespoon vanilla paste or vanilla extract

2 cups water

The Instant Pot® makes quick work of preparing this trio of classic dessert sauces, Lemon Curd (page 45), Hot Fudge Sauce (page 49), and Dulce de Leche (at left), by cooking them in canning jars on the Pressure Cook setting in record time and then storing them in the same jars to cut cleanup time.

Hot Fudge Sauce

With the Instant Pot®, whipping up this thick, shiny, chocolaty sauce is easy and fast—leaving you plenty of time to gather the vanilla ice cream, whipped cream, and cherries you'll need for a round of classic hot fudge sundaes.

In a saucepan over medium-low heat, whisk together the cream, corn syrup, butter, and chocolate chips until the chocolate and butter melt and the mixture is smooth. Add the cocoa powder, sugar, vanilla, and salt and cook, stirring constantly, until the sugar dissolves and the mixture thickens slightly, about 3 minutes. Remove from the heat and divide evenly among three ½-pint canning jars. Screw on the lids.

Pour the water into the Instant Pot® and put the trivet into the pot. Put the jars on the trivet. Lock the lid in place and turn the valve to Sealing. Press the Pressure Cook button and set the cook time for 15 minutes at high pressure.

Let the steam release naturally for 10 minutes, then turn the valve to Venting to quick-release any residual steam. Carefully remove the lid, transfer the jars to a cooling rack, and let cool for 5 minutes.

Remove the lids and serve warm. To store, re-cover the jars and refrigerate for up to 2 weeks. To reheat the sauce, warm gently in a double boiler or microwave.

Makes 3 half-pints

⅓ cup heavy cream

¾ cup light corn syrup

3 tablespoons unsalted butter

1 ⅔ cups semisweet chocolate chips

⅓ cup Dutch-process cocoa powder

½ cup sugar

2 teaspoons vanilla extract

¼ teaspoon kosher salt

1 cup water

Mixed Berry Compote

This versatile topping complements ice cream, pound cake, plain cheesecake, Greek yogurt, biscuits, waffles, pancakes, and more. You may need to adjust the amount of sugar depending on the natural sweetness of the berries.

Combine the strawberries, blueberries, raspberries, sugar, lemon juice, and orange juice and zest in the Instant Pot® and stir to coat the berries evenly. Lock the lid in place and turn the valve to Sealing. Press the Pressure Cook button and set the cook time for 3 minutes at high pressure.

Let the steam release naturally for 3 minutes, then turn the valve to Venting to quick-release any residual steam. Carefully remove the lid. Press the Cancel button to reset the program.

Press the Sauté button and cook until the berry mixture begins to boil. Stir in the cornstarch mixture and cook, stirring frequently, until the compote has thickened, about 5 minutes.

Serve warm, at room temperature, or chilled. To store, let cool, transfer to an airtight container, and refrigerate for up to 1 week.

Makes about 2½ cups

2 cups strawberries, hulled (about 12 oz)

1 cup blueberries (6 oz)

1 cup raspberries (6 oz)

¾ cup sugar

2 tablespoons fresh lemon juice

1 tablespoon fresh orange juice

2 teaspoons grated orange zest

1 tablespoon cornstarch mixed with 1 tablespoon warm water

Index

Instant Pot® Dessert

Conceived and produced by Weldon Owen International
in collaboration with Williams Sonoma, Inc.
3250 Van Ness Avenue, San Francisco, CA 94109

A WELDON OWEN PRODUCTION

1150 Brickyard Cove Road
Richmond, CA 94801
www.weldonowen.com

Printed in China
10 9 8 7 6 5 4 3 2 1

Library of Congress
Cataloging-in-Publication data is available.

ISBN 13: 978-1-68188-512-4

WELDON OWEN INTERNATIONAL

President & Publisher Roger Shaw
Associate Publisher Amy Marr
Art Director Marisa Kwek
Designer Megan Sinead Harris

Managing Editor Tarji Rodriguez
Production Manager Binh Au
Imaging Manager Don Hill

Photographer Erin Scott
Food Stylist Lillian Kang
Prop Stylist Claire Mack

ACKNOWLEDGMENTS

Weldon Owen wishes to thank the following people
for their generous support in producing this book:
Josephine Hsu, Veronica Laramie, Eve Lynch, Nicola Parisi,
Elizabeth Parson, Sharon Silva, and Nick Wolf.